March To Freedom

Remember!
Edith Singer

March To Freedom

A Memoir of the Holocaust

by
Edith Singer

True Press Publishing

Library of Congress Cataloging in Publication Data 93-94965
Singer, Edith.
March To Freedom, A Memoir of the Holocaust

ISBN 0-9638584-1-6

Cover photography by Jim Zuckerman

Printed in the United States of America

In memory of my father, Shabtai Slomovits
and my brother, Ya'akov (Yanku)

This book is dedicated to my daughters Ester and Shula,

their children Yael, Yishai, Eve and Jonathan

and to all my students who asked the questions.

Contents

Prologue

This book is about how we lived, not how we died.

When I was liberated by the Russian Army on May 8, 1945, in a small German village, I promised myself that I would not talk or think about concentration camp ever again. I knew I would never forget what happened but I wanted to push the memories out of the new life I was trying to rebuild.

Years later, I became a Hebrew School teacher. One day, an eight year old student wanted to know what the tattoo on my arm was. "Is that your phone number?" he asked. I was very upset but decided, at that moment, that I could no longer hide from or pretend to forget about my past. It was my obligation to educate the new generation about the Holocaust.

In the 1960's I started to talk to students from different kinds of schools—Jewish schools, Catholic schools, public schools and colleges. Every time I prepared to speak to a group I felt anxious and depressed.

"Again, I must tell my story. Why am I doing this?" I always asked myself. But I had made a promise to go, so I went. When I saw the reactions of the students, I knew I was doing the right thing. I felt I had taught them a very important lesson and, at the same time, I was telling my father and brother that I had not forgotten them.

As the years passed, less and less survivors remained. I realized that my stories must live on after me so I began to write them down. My family inspired and encouraged me.

It was not easy. Every story took me back to Auschwitz and *Taucha. After completing each story I stopped for a few months until I could write again.

One day, I looked over a previously written story and discovered that I had written down details I thought I had forgotten. By writing down my experiences I let go of some of the painful memories.

I hope that the readers of this book will gain a better understanding of the Holocaust and will unite in the struggle against evil so that it may never happen again.

*A labor camp, not to be confused with Dachau, the death camp

Before The War

LILLY, FRIEDA, YANKU, SHABTAI AND EDITH, 1933

CHUST, MAIN STREET

The Ghetto In Chust

I was born in Chust, Czechoslovakia between the two World Wars. Chust was a small town of 20,000 Gentiles and 5,000 Jews.

I was raised in a religious home. My father was in the lumber business and we lived a comfortable, middle-class life. At home, we spoke Yiddish, Hungarian and German. At school, we spoke Czech. When my parents were born at the beginning of the century, Chust was part of the Austro-Hungarian Empire so they spoke Hungarian and German and taught us too. After World War I our part of Hungary became Czechoslovakia.

My earliest memories of public school were associated with anti-Semitism. The non-Jewish students and teachers did not hide their prejudice. Even in kindergarten, the Jewish children were forced to sit at separate tables at the back of the room.

One day, I came to school with a bad case of laryngitis. As soon as the music teacher realized that I was hoarse she called on me to sing a solo. I pleaded with her to excuse me but she insisted that I stand in front of the class and sing, humiliating me to the point of tears. The entire class laughed and teased me. Another teacher ruined my straight A report card by giving me an undeserved B in sewing.

I remember only one teacher, Miss Pearl, an older woman, who was kind to the Jewish children. She stopped her regular lesson to lecture the class about the evils of prejudice. But this did not help because the next day the teasing, the name-calling and the beatings in the school yard continued. Whenever we were hurt we went to Miss Pearl and she comforted us. We loved her for her kindness during this difficult time.

In 1939 World War II broke out and Hitler gave our part of Czechoslovakia, known as Carpatorusse, back to Hungary. Overnight, the language of instruction in my school changed from Czech to Hungarian. This was not a major problem for the children because we learned fast.

With the Hungarian occupation our lives changed completely. The government enacted all types of anti-Semitic laws. Our lives became increasingly difficult. At first, all Jews in public office were fired. All private businesses owned by Jews were taken away by the authorities and given to non-Jews.

Every few weeks new restrictions came out. We had to bring all our radios, bicycles, sewing machines and any other machines that had any value to City Hall. All these items were distributed among the non-Jewish population of Chust.

We managed to hide our radio. Some of our neighbors came over at night and we listened to the London broadcast. If the news was good we believed it. If it was bad we told ourselves it must be German propaganda.

Some Jews who did not have Hungarian citizenship papers were expelled from Chust and sent to Poland. A few managed to sneak back to our town and told us horrible stories about what was happening there. Jews were forced to dig their own mass graves and were then shot. Camps surrounded by electrified wires were set up. I did not believe this was true and would not accept that this could happen to our family. But my parents were worried and afraid.

I was in the last class that was allowed to complete Junior High School. All the other Jewish students who were one class level below me were not allowed to attend public school anymore. Parents set up private schools in their homes so that their children could continue their studies.

Outside of school, life was hard too. We never knew what would happen next. Every Jewish man, woman and child was open prey for the anti-Semites.

One day, my father came home with his beard shaved off. It was the first time in my life that I saw my father without his beard. He wore a beard for religious reasons. When we asked him what happened he told us that a Hungarian soldier grabbed him on the street, took him to a barber shop and ordered the barber, "Shave the beard off this Jew!"

Often, on a train or bus, a non-Jew would demand from a Jew to give up his seat or move to the last compartment. Many times a drunk who needed money would grab a Jew on the street, take him to the police station and lie to an officer saying, "This Jew took my money!" The police officer would order the Jew to give the drunkard all the money he had. The innocent man was then beaten and thrown into jail for a few days without even being questioned.

All these restrictions made our lives difficult but we were still together in our homes and we were not hungry. This went on until March of 1944. I was sixteen years old.

One morning we woke up and realized that the German army had occupied all of Hungary. At that point our lives changed rapidly from bad to tragic.

The first thing the Germans did was arrest all the Jewish leaders and rabbis. Some non-Jews who knew the Jewish population of Chust, and who collaborated with the Nazis, prepared this list of leaders. We were ordered to sew yellow stars on our clothing. A curfew from dusk to dawn was enforced on the Jewish population. Food was rationed only for the Jews and Kosher meat was forbidden. These orders came so fast that we had no time to grasp what was happening.

Whatever the Germans did in other occupied countries over the course of several years they accomplished in Hungary in just a few weeks. After only one month of the German occupation we were told to take with us whatever we could fit on a wagon and go to the ghetto.

The ghetto in Chust consisted of a few blocks of homes enclosed by a high, barbed-wire fence. Five thousand Jews were forced to live in this small area.

My family was assigned to a house that belonged to one of our cousins. It was an average, three-bedroom house. Close to one hundred people lived in this house. My parents, Frieda and Shabtai, my twenty year old sister Lilly, my eighteen year old brother Yanku and I were in one small room with two additional families—fourteen people in all. We brought our mattresses from home and spread them out on the floor at night. All three families slept one next to the other. During the day we piled the mattresses up in a corner so that we could move around in the room and get to our suitcases. When we wanted to change clothes we had to hold up a make-shift curtain for privacy. But, our family was still together and we were not hungry.

We brought all our food from home and the mothers cooked and even competed with each other—who could make a better meal. We ate together and after the meals the girls washed the dishes. Often, the adults fought with each other over trivial things. Everyone's nerves were on edge.

When the Germans were not around the adults gathered

the children in one of the rooms and taught them whatever they could. A doctor taught biology, an engineer taught math, a rabbi taught Hebrew. They wanted their children to go on with their schooling.

The older boys tried to learn some self-defense tactics to protect themselves against confrontations with the Nazis. My brother Yanku was one of the leaders of this group. Whatever he knew or read about in books he taught to the younger boys. They did not know that they would never have a chance to protect themselves against what the Germans had planned for them.

Every morning, officers from the *Gestapo came to the ghetto. When they arrived, everybody immediately busied themselves. We grabbed a broom and swept our rooms or the yard outside. We had to show them that we worked.

Each time the Gestapo came all the men had to line up. The fear was great because we never knew what they wanted. Usually, they picked a group of young men and took them to work somewhere outside the city. They were brought back late in the evening.

One day, Yanku was picked to go to work. My father was so upset he did not talk the whole day. He paced back and forth from our cramped room to the gate of the ghetto. It became dark and Yanku was not back yet. That day the first rumors of taking us "away" surfaced, fueling my father's panic. Finally, the group of young men returned to the ghetto. My father saw Yanku, ran to him and burst out crying. I never saw my father cry before. Later, he told my mother that he was afraid Yanku would not return in time to be with us when we were taken away from the ghetto.

In the beginning of May 1944, four weeks after we had arrived in the ghetto, we were told to take with us only what we could carry and march to the train station.

The march to the train station was a very sad one. Everyone carried as much as they could hold in their two hands. The children held on tightly to their dolls and Teddy

*The German secret state police

bears. Five thousand people, young and old, carrying all kinds of suitcases, knapsacks, baskets and wrapped bundles, marched in silence.

The walk was about three miles long. The streets were abandoned. The non-Jewish population of Chust hid inside their houses. Our neighbors—people we had worked with, grown up with, gone to school with, and played with—became invisible. They did not come out to say goodbye, to give us something for our journey or to promise to take care of our homes until we returned. Nothing. Empty streets. Only a large, silent group of Jews walked to the station accompanied by the Hungarian police and the Gestapo.

At the station we were searched for hidden money, jewelry and other valuables. I saw people frantically emptying their pockets and throwing money on the street, afraid that if they were found with any they would be beaten.

Yanku was searched and money that my mother had sewn into his jacket lapel was found. The Hungarian policeman began to hit him.

"Please, don't hurt my son," my father pleaded. "I have more money. I'll give you everything. Just don't hit him." My father undid his hernia belt, opened up a seam and gave the policeman all he had.

Then we were pushed into cattle trains that took us away from Chust to the unknown.

Arrival In Auschwitz

The locomotive pulled a long row of cattle cars behind it. The cargo—Jews. We were being transported from Hungary to a destination unknown to us. I was in one of the cattle cars with my family, along with eighty other people from my hometown, Chust.

It was extremely crowded and stuffy inside. The only fresh air came from two tiny windows at the top of the cattle car. We were given a few buckets—some were filled with water and the others were for toilet use. When we had to use the toilet, someone would hold a blanket up for privacy.

We brought food with us for the journey but nobody could eat. I remember a bag of butter cookies my mother had baked "for the road." Later, in concentration camp, during the longest year of my life, I often thought about those cookies. I could not forgive myself for not eating more of them when I could.

For the first two days, the trains were guarded by the Hungarian police. Then the Gestapo and the *SS took over. They rode on top of the train with their machine guns aimed at us.

The cattle cars were opened once a day to empty the buckets and to get fresh water. Every time the guards opened the doors they took two or three hostages from each car. We heard shots but could not see what was happening. The Germans demanded money and jewelry for the hostages' return. Even though we had been thoroughly searched before entering the trains, some people managed to hide a few valuables. Those who had hidden money or jewelry gave it up to save the hostages.

After four days of traveling, the train stopped again. But this time the doors were not opened for water or bucket changes. We waited one hour, two, three and then we stopped counting.

The hot, stale air, the stench, the crying of children, the moaning of the sick, and the uncertainty were unbearable. Night fell and we were still inside the train. We remained locked inside without fresh water for over twenty four hours. We did not know where we were and what awaited us. We heard talking outside but could not reach the two little windows to look out and see what was going on.

Finally, the doors of the cattle cars were opened. We all rushed forward to get some fresh air and see what was going on outside. We saw German SS soldiers, officers, and men in gray and blue striped clothing.

I saw a large sign with the word "Auschwitz" on it. I did not know what it meant. It was the first time I saw this name, a name I was never to forget. Under it were the words *Arbiet Macht Frei* (Work Makes You Free). It made no sense to me.

The elite military units of the Nazi Party who used terror and destruction to achieve their goals

My father stood in the open door looking around silently and then said to us: "I see people in striped uniforms, like in a prison. But at least they are alive. We will obey all the rules and we will survive." I looked at my father's sad face and only then did I understand his fears.

"*Raus, schnell!* Out, quickly!" the Germans shouted at us. We had to jump out of the trains onto the ground, three feet below. It was most difficult for the elderly and the sick. No ladders or platforms were set up but we helped each other as much as we could.

We all had some kind of baggage with us—a knapsack, a suitcase, a small parcel. As we jumped down, we heard the next order: "Put your belongings there!" I looked "there" and saw a huge mountain of baggage—all shapes and sizes.

"How will I recognize my bags if they are all thrown over there?" I thought. I did not know that they would never be returned to me.

"Men here, women there!" was the next command. Everything happened so quickly and unexpectedly that we did not even have the chance to say goodbye to one another. This was the first separation of families.

Standing in line with all the women and children, I looked over at the men's side. I wanted another glance, another word from my father and brother. Suddenly, my tall father looked so small, so frightened. His confident, warm smile that always comforted me as a child was gone. For a moment our eyes met. My father and brother said something but I could not hear them—I was too far away. All I could do was wave, unaware that this was the last time I would ever see them.

The men in the striped clothing herded us towards the main gate. Their job was to process the new *transports. Whenever they got close to us they whispered in Yiddish, *"Gibt die kleine kinder zu die alte mentschen."* Give the small children to the old people. I understood the words but I did not know what they meant.

*Nazi term for train loads of people arriving in Auschwitz

These men were the "old-timers" of Auschwitz. They were prisoners who knew what was going on and they tried to warn us.

The mothers panicked and clutched their children closer to them. The line kept moving.

"Gibt die kleine kinder zu die alte mentschen!" the prisoners insisted. "You will have to work but the old folks can take care of the children. Give them, quickly, before it's too late."

They could not tell the mothers the truth. The old-timers knew that women with young children, the elderly and the sick were to be killed right away. Hesitantly, some mothers handed their children over to their older relatives believing they would be safe, fed and taken care of. By separating the mothers from their children the old-timers managed to save a few young women.

My favorite aunt, Judith, held her baby in her arms. Her four other children clung tightly to her skirt. She would not leave them. "I cannot, I cannot!" she cried in anguish. They were all sent to the left side, to the gas chambers.

We moved closer and closer to the main gate. I held on to my mother and sister. Facing us was a high ranking SS officer. He was tall with dark hair, wearing white gloves and an impeccable SS uniform. He held a small pointer in his hand and smiled at us. He was the most handsome man I had ever seen— he was Dr. Mengele.

With a slight movement of his pointer he indicated to the right or to the left. This little movement of his gloved hand determined our fate; right was life, left was death.

He looked at my aunt, Hankaneni, who stood next to us and asked her, *"Wie alt bist du?"* How old are you?

"Funf und dreisig." Thirty-five, she answered quickly. She was close to fifty. Her fast thinking saved her life.

My mother, sister and I passed Dr. Mengele's selection without questions. This was the first time, but not the last, that we would meet Dr. Mengele, "The Angel of Death."

On our way to the *Entlausing* (delousing) building we passed a small podium where several prisoners played classical music. I did not know why.* We continued marching and saw strange looking people behind barbed wires. They were women, but we were not sure at first as their heads were shaved. They were screaming and motioning wildly to us. "Give us your food! Throw us whatever you have. You won't be able to hold on to anything. Please, give us some bread!" We did not understand and we did not believe them. I thought they were the insane inmates of the camp. Several hours later we understood. They were not crazy. They were like we were before and now we were like them.

We arrived at a huge concrete building. In the first room we were told to undress and stand in line. I was shocked and embarrassed. I tried in vain to cover myself with my arms. This was the first time we stood naked while SS soldiers and male prisoners shuffled us from room to room. We were told to leave all our clothing behind except for our shoes.

A line of female old-timers holding hair clippers shaved our heads and the hair from the rest of our bodies. We were pushed to the next room. We put our shoes by the wall and went back into the center of the room. Suddenly, cold water sprayed us from the ceiling. We did not have soap. The shower lasted a few minutes. In the next room another group of old-timers sprayed us with disinfectant powder. At the last stop, before going outside again, we received clothing; one pair of underwear and one dress. With this strange clothing and shaved heads we hardly recognized one another. My mother, sister and I held each other tightly so as not to get separated in the mass of anonymous bodies.

We were standing outside when we were ordered to stand *Appell* (roll call) for the first time. We had to line up quickly, five people to a row. The SS guards counted us and then we were taken to Camp C.

The Nazis used music to distract the new arrivals and allay their suspicions. It was also for their own enjoyment.

We were exhausted and hungry. "Maybe now we will receive some warm food and go to bed," I thought. But in Camp C we stood *Appell* for several more hours.

Our *Blockelteste*, Eitu—a Jewish girl, an old-timer and head of our barracks—told us about Auschwitz. We did not believe the horrors she told us about. "You were still in your homes, with your family when I was already here. You had enough food when I was hungry," she screamed at us.

Finally, we were given our first meal—a piece of black, mud-like bread, a tiny square of margarine and one thin slice of salami. We could not eat the bread and left it on the ground. The old-timers immediately snatched it up. Very quickly we learned that there was no choice in food and we ate whatever we were given.

We entered a huge, empty barracks. There were no beds yet. One thousand women slept on the bare concrete floor. We had to lie on top of each other. Sleep was impossible. Just as we dozed off someone started to scream. Then another woman screamed, then another and soon the hysterical screaming of a thousand women filled the barracks. I held my mother and sister's hand. "We are not going to scream," I told them. The *Blockelteste* came out from her private corner and shouted at us to quiet down.

At 3:00 a.m. we were roused by the *Blockelteste* yelling at us to get up and out. It was pitch black and very cold when our first day in Auschwitz began.

Appell

It was still dark when we were ordered to stand *Appell*. The Germans counted us twice a day—once, early in the morning and again in the late afternoon—before we received our daily ration of food.

There was an open area between the rows of barracks specifically designed for *Appell*. We formed lines—five people to a row; two columns of five hundred women from each barracks.

During the morning *Appell* it was extremely cold. We stood very close to each other, using our body heat for warmth. There was always pushing and yelling because everyone tried to be in the middle of the five person row to get the maximum warmth from bodies on both sides. My mother always said to the people in our line, "I will stand at the end of our line as long as you let my two daughters stay in the middle." She was so small and fragile yet she always wanted to shelter us from the cold.

Later, after I was separated from my mother and sister, I decided to stand at the end of the line so that I could toughen myself for the future. If, one day, I would not be in the middle of the line I wanted to be strong enough to survive the cold on the outside of the line. But after one try on the outside I was so cold and miserable that I fought my way back to the middle. I decided that I would harden myself for the cold when I had no other choice.

We stood *Appell* for several hours, our shivering bodies huddled together. Slowly, the darkness faded and the sun came out.

"The SS are coming! Straighten up!" The warning spread quickly through the rows. A group of thirty SS officers marched into our camp—one officer for each barracks. They had a very efficient system for counting us. They took one look and could see immediately if there were five people to a row. The counting itself went very fast: five-ten-fifteen-twenty. If the prisoners' attendance matched their roll call numbers the *Appell* was over. But if even one prisoner was missing—if someone was too sick to come out, if someone was asleep in a dark corner of the barracks, or if someone had died during the night—then all 30,000 prisoners had to stand or kneel for hours until the missing prisoner was found.

At first, the kneeling was only a humiliating discomfort but as the hours passed it became physical torture. The gravel cut into our knees. We tucked our dresses under our knees but this only made it worse because later we had to tear the dress off of our bloodied skin. Our bodies ached but if someone tried to move or shift position an SS guard or *Kapo* would be there immediately with their whips on our backs.

The next day our knees were infected and swollen. There

*A prisoner put in charge of other prisoners

was nothing we could do, only suffer silently.

The afternoon *Appell* started a few hours after lunch. We had barely settled into our bunk beds when we were ordered to go outside again.

The sun was high and our shaved heads got sunburned. Our lips got burned and cracked. By the time the SS came to count us it was five o'clock in the afternoon. It was unbearable standing in line for so many hours. The weak and sick women sank to the ground and sat on the gravel.

One SS officer came by every day just before the actual counting. The warning spread. "He is coming!" Quickly, we helped up those who were sitting and we all straightened up. He walked by our lines slowly, with a big stick in his hand and a mocking smile on his face. He picked several women out from our lines and beat them severely.

"Why did you sit down! You know you have to stand and wait until you are counted!" he screamed at them.

If some of us tried to defend the women saying they did not sit down, the beatings became worse. We could not understand how he always picked the right women—the ones who had actually sat down—since everyone was standing by the time he got to our lines. Finally, we figured out that he looked at the back of our dresses and if he saw dirt on them he knew who had sat on the ground. From that point on we always made sure to brush off our dresses.

One evening after *Appell* we were told to undress and line up again inside the barracks. As we moved down the line we were sprayed with disinfectant. Then we were unexpectedly given a clean set of clothing; one dress and one pair of underwear. It was a matter of luck what size we received. Lilly and I got dresses in our size but my mother received a very small one that did not even cover her body. We told her to sneak into the line again and try to get another dress. She did but was caught by Eitu and got slapped brutally across the face. The blood gushed from her cracked lips.

"Why did you hit our mother?" Lilly screamed at Eitu.

"Look what you did! Her lips are bleeding!" I yelled.

Eitu was enraged and just about to hit us too when her sister came to our rescue. She took us aside and washed the blood off my mother's face with a clean rag. Without a word, Eitu gave my mother a larger dress.

Every day after *Appell*, Mother, Lilly and I were grateful that we returned to our barracks together. We tried not to think of the days ahead and what might happen to us. I prayed for the day when I would not have to stand in line for *Appell*.

◆

Ever since then, I have an aversion for standing in lines, especially for anything that is not essential, such as movies, amusement parks, and restaurants.

Lunch

Morning *Appell* was over, but we were not allowed to return to the barracks until they had been cleaned by a few appointed prisoners. While they were cleaning we waited outside. There were several cold water faucets in the camp. Everyone tried to push their way to the faucets to wash up a little or drink from their cupped palms.

At mid-morning we were allowed to return to the barracks. We went to the bunk beds where we could lie on one side or we sat with our legs tucked under our chin, and did nothing. We could not talk to each other as the *Blockelteste* demanded silence.

It seemed like an eternity until we were told to go outside

again. Lunch time was approaching. Thirty thousand women lined up in several rows to receive their meager bowl of soup. In this soup, the Germans put bromide, a tranquilizer.

When we first arrived in Auschwitz we were terrified. Someone would cry out, "Look, there is gas! They are poisoning us!" We all screamed and cried in terror. Mass hysteria could break out at any time.

Two or three weeks after our arrival the screaming stopped and all the women stopped menstruating. We were told by the old-timers that the bromide did this.

The old-timers who worked in the kitchen brought out large kettles of soup. A few women who had somehow obtained a small bowl risked a beating by running to the open kettle to scoop up some soup. It was a difficult and dangerous undertaking but hunger overtook all reasoning. The rest of us—thousands of hungry women—waited in line as military canteens were passed out. They were collected after lunch.

As we moved along the line the excitement grew. Which part of the soup will I get? Will it be from the top of the kettle and very watery? Or will it be from the bottom of the kettle, a bit thicker with some small pieces of vegetables in it? But no matter what part of the soup we got it was always horrible. The vegetables were not washed and we felt the grit of sand between our teeth. It took us a few days to learn to eat this soup. My mother forced herself to eat her soup and some of ours. She told us that she liked it so that in the evening she could give us half of her bread, saying she had eaten enough at lunch.

Some prisoners snuck into other lines to try to get a second helping. If they were caught they were beaten by the SS guards who watched us during lunch time. They walked among the prisoners with their whips ready. They enjoyed seeing how far a hungry person would go for a little extra watery soup.

Occasionally, the SS guards would let a few prisoners go for a second bowl of soup and just as they started to eat, the guards would jump on the surprised victims and beat them. Sometimes they let the prisoners finish the second helping and then attacked them.

In the beginning we did not understand how the SS guards knew who had eaten twice. In time, we realized that when the SS saw two canteens next to one prisoner or when someone came to take soup and her dish was not clean, they knew she was getting a second bowl of soup. All these tricks had to be learned to avoid being caught and punished. It was part of the struggle for survival.

Lunch was over but we were still hungry. Again, we were left outside. We had nothing to do but feel our hunger and misery and wait for the next order.

Wandering around the camp, we met some relatives, friends or neighbors who were in other barracks. We talked and sought comfort from each other. Once I overheard some older women talking.

"Do you realize where we are? We will never get out of here alive!"

"Yes, I know where we are," the other women answered. "Through the gate we came in and through the chimney we will go out."

I got scared. I knew I could not go on if I was so terrified all the time. I wanted to survive. I had to find a way of going on, a way to resist the Germans and stay alive.

"I will not listen to people who are pessimistic and who do not believe in a future," I thought to myself. "If God wants me to die than it can happen any time, anywhere, even after the war, even on my way home. But if God wants me to live no German or anyone else can harm me."

The day passed slowly. We were still hungry and still left standing outside. By this time the sun was burning high in the sky. We looked for a shady place to stand but the few places next to the walls of the barracks were already occupied.

Then the shouting began again. "Everybody inside. Quickly! Move!" We ran into the barracks and crawled onto the bunk beds. Lunch at Auschwitz was over.

Sleeping

We were sleeping fitfully on our wooden bunk beds when the lights in the barracks went on and Eitu the *Blockelteste* and her *Kapos* shouted at us.

"*Aufstein, raus, schnell*! Get up! Everybody outside! Fast!" We had to jump down from our bunk beds and run outside.

The bunk beds were three levels high—bare wooden planks with no mattresses, no blankets and no pillows. Fifteen women slept on each level—seven in one direction, seven in the opposite direction and one person lay across the middle on top of everyone's legs. We only had room to lie on one side. If one person wanted to turn to the other side all fifteen women had to turn also. Lying on one side for hours, without moving was unbearable. Our bones ached, our legs cramped and numbness spread through our bodies.

"Please, let's turn to the other side," my sister Lilly said one night.

"No, not yet!" answered the woman next to her. "I am still all right and my sister is asleep already."

Lilly waited in pain and then begged again. "Let's turn now, please!" No one moved. Lilly could not wait any longer and started to kick her neighbors until everyone turned to the other side.

Almost every night an upper bunk collapsed sending the startled women crashing down to the second level and then to the bottom level. They got hurt and started to scream. Eitu rushed in shouting at everyone to be quiet and ordered the bunk bed fixed. Two of her helpers brought in a hammer and nails and repaired the bunk bed.

In spite of the terrible sleeping conditions, sleep was the only escape we had from the reality of Auschwitz. When we slept we did not feel the hunger, the pain and the misery.

Sometimes, when Eitu was away from the barracks, we talked quietly to each other. We talked about our families, our homes, and our lives before Auschwitz.

One young woman, Klari, told us that she had married her high school sweetheart but he was taken to a forced labor camp right after the wedding ceremony. She never saw him again.

"Do you mean to say that you are a married woman and still a virgin?" we teased her. For a few moments we laughed together and from that day on we called Klari the "Virgin Wife."

It made us think about our own romantic future. Would we live to meet a young man, to know what love is, to get married and have children?

There was a Jewish Hungarian woman in her early forties who read palms. She was a friendly and optimistic person, always predicting a bright future for everyone who came to her. I watched her reading the palms of other women and then I too stretched out my hand. She looked at it closely.

"Oh, darling, you have a very long life line," she said.

"What does that mean?" I asked.

"You will live a long time, eighty or ninety years."

"You mean I will survive this hell? I'll go home to my family? I'll eat a lot of bread?" I asked excitedly.

"Of course, darling," she reassured me. "You will find your family and one day you will have your own children and you will be happy again."

I thanked her, walked away and believed what she told me.

Sometimes we were lucky and had pleasant dreams. One night, I dreamed that I was home with my family for the Sabbath dinner. The candles flickered in the silver candlesticks. The large *challas* were under the embroidered cover. Dressed in our best Sabbath clothes, we stood around the table and listened to my father bless the wine and *challah*. Just as I reached out to get my thick slice of *challah* I felt an elbow jabbing me in the stomach.

"What's going on? Why are you hitting me?" I asked the girl lying next to me.

"You stretched out your hand and almost poked my eye out!" she answered angrily.

I tried to go back to sleep and enter my dream world of home again but instead I heard the screaming of the *Blockelteste*, "*Aufstein, aufstein!*"

Quickly, we put on our shoes which we used as pillows. We slept in our only dress. The shouting became louder and louder. We wanted so badly to hold on to our precious moments of sleep but we were ordered to run outside where we joined the thousands of women from the other barracks.

Eitu stood in the open doorway with a large stick in her hand, pushing, shouting, and hitting us as we ran out. It was impossible for one thousand women to get out of the barracks at once. Everyone tried to be in the middle of the pushing crowd to avoid the painful blows of Eitu's stick.

There were no SS guards around at this time. Eitu did not have to impress them with her cruelty, yet she hit us anyway.

It was dark and very cold outside. Only the lights on top of the electrified fences were lit, reminding the prisoners that the slightest touch of the wires meant instant electrocution. In this eerie light thousands of women moved toward the latrine.

Latrine

One barracks at the end of our camp was the latrine.
Inside, three long, raised concrete rows with hundreds of holes
cut into them served as our toilets. Thirty thousand women had
to use this latrine within a very short period of time.

It was dark inside. I held my mother and sister's hand so as
not to lose them. People were pushing and screaming trying to
find an unoccupied hole. There was no toilet paper. Often the
top was soiled with excrement.

One day, after the morning *Appell*, Eitu looked for prisoners to do some work. Without knowing the nature of the work I
volunteered.

Twenty girls from our barracks were taken to the latrine.

Two *Kapos* were waiting for us. They gave us large shovels and several wheel barrows and told us to clean the latrine. We looked at each other in shock. I almost vomited from the stench but I knew there was no turning back. I took a shovel and started to work.

"I don't care what kind of work it is," I thought to myself as I shoveled the excrement. It was better to work than to languish in the barracks dreaming of food, waiting for the next order, and wasting away.

When the cleaning was done I was told to stand at the doorway and not let anyone in. Many prisoners came by and wanted to use the latrine but I had to say, "No."

A woman clutching her stomach and doubled over in pain came running to the gate. "May I go inside?" she asked me anxiously.

"No, you cannot," I answered.

"But I have to. I'm sick," she pleaded.

"You know that no one is allowed to go in at this time," I told her.

She did not leave. She looked at me with sad eyes. "Please let me in. Please!" she begged.

Her voice sounded familiar. I looked at her closely. Even with her shaved head and her body shrunken from starvation, I recognized her. She had been my high school science teacher just a few months ago, before we were taken to Auschwitz. She had been a good-looking, friendly woman and her students had loved her. She stood before me in a badly fitting, dirty dress. She had no socks and her shoes were torn.

"Margitneni?" I asked in a friendlier tone.

She looked at me in amazement. She did not recognize me. She did not ask how I knew her. "Yes, I am Margitneni. Will you let me in?"

I looked around. No one was watching. I opened the door. "Quick!" I whispered, and she ran into the latrine.

Inside our barracks at the far end, eight buckets were set up for toilet use. They served the one thousand women prisoners when they were not allowed to go outside to the latrine. At other times, the same buckets were used for drinking water.

We asked Eitu to let us use the buckets. "If you behave and stay very quiet I will let you go later," she told us.

We tried to stay quiet but some of the women cried out in pain, "Please, let me go! I cannot wait any longer. I am sick."

"Quiet!" Eitu shouted. "I told you to behave." Finally, after endless waiting, she announced, "Line up, don't push and don't talk."

Some of the women jumped down from their bunk beds. The weak and sick ones had to be helped down.

There was always a long line for the buckets. Many women who had dysentery could not wait for their turn and soiled themselves and the area around them. This always brought a beating from Eitu or her helpers.

One morning, my sister and I stood in line waiting to use the buckets. We were at the end of the line and had to wait for a long time. I felt as if I was going to explode but I was too scared to let go. An excruciating pain racked my body. I burst out crying.

"Hold on," Lilly told me knowing what would happen if I did not. She held my hand and reassured me over and over, "We are almost there."

Somehow, I made it to the buckets and avoided a beating.

Organizieren

At first, I thought it was just a bad nightmare. I would soon wake up and find myself at home in my own bed, covered with a big feather comforter, my family around me, and plenty of food in the kitchen. But after several days in Auschwitz, I realized that this was not a bad dream but a terrible and cruel reality. My previous life in the little town of Chust was now just images that lived in my memory. Sometimes I wondered if it ever existed—it seemed so far away, so unreachable. The constant hunger, the endless waiting from one order to the next, the milling around with nothing to do—that became my new reality.

I was very hungry in Auschwitz—so hungry that nothing

else was on my mind except food. We received two meager meals a day. For lunch, we got a bowl of watery vegetable soup. The evening meal consisted of a small piece of dark, coarse bread, one thin slice of salami and a square of margarine. It was never enough. I always fantasized about having enough bread to feel full. I had a little prayer: if I am to die here, I would rather die today than tomorrow so that I will be hungry one day less.

I, like many other prisoners, was always looking for some extra food. When new prisoners arrived and were marched through the main gate, we asked them to throw us whatever food they still had with them. We knew that all their possessions would be taken away but they did not know this and most of them held on to their belongings.

We had various means of obtaining extra food, shoes, a scarf, a needle and thread and other necessities. This was called *"organizieren"*—to organize something for oneself. Standing around the kitchen when a truck delivered carrots and turnips and snatching the fallen ones was called *organizieren*. Receiving a little extra soup for helping the girl who served lunch was *organizieren*. To grab a piece of clothing from an open storage building was *organizieren*. As long as the object obtained was not stolen from another prisoner it was *organizieren*.

Electrified barbed wire fences separated one camp from the other. We often stood by the fences looking for relatives or any bits of information about family or friends.

Camp B was known as the "Czech Camp" as it was occupied by prisoners transported from Theresienstadt concentration camp in Czechoslovakia. One day, I saw an older man from the Czech camp standing by the fence holding a woolen scarf. A woman from my camp, holding a half ration of bread, was bargaining with him. After they agreed on the trade the man threw the scarf to her but it caught on the electrified wires. As he reached out to get his scarf his right hand touched the wire. He screamed out in pain but could not free his hand.

Slowly, he lifted his left hand, placed it carefully between the wires and pried his fingers loose one by one. He freed his hand and ran away, leaving the scarf behind.

Another time, I saw a group of women standing in a circle. I pushed closer to see what was going on. A young girl was doing acrobatic exercises. As we watched her, we forgot for a few minutes where we were and how hungry we felt. Someone gave her a bite of bread for her little performance.

Once, I heard beautiful singing coming from the SS living quarters. A woman prisoner was singing under their window. She had been a famous opera singer in Budapest. She sang in the hope that one of the SS officers would hear her and reward her with something to eat. After several songs a door opened. An SS woman came out and gave her a piece of bread, yelling, "Take this and go away. Don't come back or you will be in big trouble." The opera singer thanked her and ran away. She never sang there again.

On another occasion a woman came up to me. She had a little piece of bread in her hand. "Are you Shabtai Slomovits' daughter from Chust?" she asked me.

"Yes I am. Who are you?" I said.

"It is not important who I am. I knew your father and he once did a big favor for my family." She gave me the bread and disappeared into the crowd of prisoners.

I never found out who she was or how she recognized me, but I discovered that my father's goodness reached me even here. I had not seen my father since the day we arrived in Auschwitz when the men were separated from the women.

In the last week of July 1944 I was separated from my mother and sister. I was sent to the Czech camp adjacent to Camp C but I was still able to see and talk to them through the fence every day.

One morning, I met Lilly at the fence. She had no shirt on and covered herself with her arms, crying hopelessly.

"Lilly, what happened to you? Where is your shirt?" I asked her.

"Someone stole it while I was washing myself at the water pipe. What will I do now?" she cried.

"Wait here," I told her. "I'll see what I can find." I had no idea what to do. All I knew was that my big sister was crying, cold and scared. I wandered around the camp talking to the other prisoners, asking for help. A woman pointed out the clothing storage area where piles of clothes, stripped from the arriving prisoners, filled the barracks.

I lingered around this area waiting for an opportunity to get nearer to the clothes. When no SS guards or *Kapos* were around I sneaked in, snatched the first piece of clothing I saw and ran out. I did not stop running until I reached Lilly at the fence. She was still crying, covering her body. I looked at the rumpled cloth in my hand. It was a shirt! I pushed it carefully through the fence. "Here, Lillyke, don't cry. And next time be more careful."

Birkenau was the main storage camp of Auschwitz. Mountains of clothes, shoes, luggage, eyeglasses, pots and pans, sacks of shorn hair, books, and toys filled the entire camp—the last possessions taken from millions of Jews arriving at Auschwitz.

Every prisoner dreamed of being sent to work in Birkenau where the possibilities for *organizieren* were better. One day, I and a group of thirty other women were sent to Birkenau for the day, loading giant bundles of clothes onto trucks destined for Germany. It was hard work but it was better than spending endless days languishing in the camp.

On our way back to the Czech camp I passed a mountain of shoes. It was getting cold. Winter was approaching. I looked down at my own worn shoes. I did not have much time to think. Quickly, I grabbed two shoes and hid them under my shirt. Just then, we were ordered to march back to our camp.

"Where are you from?" the prisoners from Birkenau called out to us as we marched past them. We were always thirsting for any information about our relatives—who was still alive, who was sent away from Auschwitz, who had heard any news.

"Do you know anyone from Munkacs, Chust, Solotfene?" a young woman asked me.

"Yes, I am from Chust," I said.

"Do you know Ella Heinfeld?" she asked.

"Yes, but…" and before I could reply she pressed a pair of shoes into my hands.

"Please give these to Ella. Tell her they are from Magda, her cousin."

The SS and *Kapos* were pushing us along and shouting "*Schnell*, quickly!" I did not have the chance to tell her that Ella, who was pregnant, had been taken away yesterday with all the other pregnant women. I hid the shoes under my skirt.

Now I was in a dilemma. I was given a pair of shoes for someone who no longer existed. Returning them to Magda was impossible for I had already left her far behind.

My heart pounded as we approached the gate. The shoes were bulging under my clothes. Will the SS search me? What will they do to me if they find the shoes? Will they beat me? Will they kill me? There was no search. This was my lucky day.

Arriving at my barracks I took out the treasure I had snatched from the pile; a pair of mismatched men's shoes—one shoe was size ten, the other size eleven. Although I wore a size five it did not matter. These shoes would keep my feet dry and warm during the coming winter. The other pair of shoes that Magda had given me were lined with flannel and had a modern zipper in place of laces. I gave them to my mother so she could slip them on quickly when ordered to run outside for *Appell*. I had no shoes for Lilly.

One day I was talking to Petyu Kreindler, a girl from my hometown and as always, we talked about food. We came up with a plan for organizing some extra food.

We sewed two small sacks out of pieces of cloth from our

dresses. Petyu had a pot with a handle. Late at night, when everyone was sleeping, we slipped out of our barracks and crept along the walls praying that the guards would not see us.

We got to the kitchen area and waited in the darkness. We heard trucks approaching. They came every night dumping large mounds of vegetables onto the ground. Prisoners carried the potatoes, carrots and turnips into the kitchen. Petyu and I were ready. The moment the vegetables were left unguarded Petyu grabbed a potful of potatoes, ran back to me and emptied them into the sack. Then it was my turn to run, grab a potful of potatoes and bring them to Petyu. We repeated this several times until both our sacks were full.

We returned to our barracks and divided up the potatoes evenly. There was not much time left for sleeping, but having the potatoes and the hope of trading them for extra bread the next day compensated for the loss of sleep.

The next morning I went to the fence of the men's camp. The old-timers had a small stove for cooking there. A man traded a loaf of bread for my potatoes. I had to be very careful not to get electrocuted and not to be spotted by the SS as I passed the sack of potatoes through the fence.

I divided my loaf of bread evenly into three parts and hid them under my clothes until I saw my mother and sister waiting on the other side of the fence. Avoiding contact with the wires I passed the two portions of bread through the fence to them.

The very thought that I could lessen their hunger and my own gave me the strength to continue organizing and stay alive.

Selections

"**M**engele is coming! Mengele is coming!" The news rumbled through the camp like a thunder clap. My mother, my sister and I held on to each other tightly.

We ran to line up. Mengele's coming meant selections. He chose people for different purposes, separating families and friends. What will the selection be for this time? Will he pick people to leave Auschwitz for slave labor in factories all over Europe? Will he choose pregnant women for medical experiments? Will he select the pretty girls and send them to the soldiers on the front? Will he ask those who play piano to step forward and then assign them to latrine duty? Will he choose the weak and sickly and send them to the gas chambers? We never knew but we were always afraid.

Whenever he came to our camp a group of SS officers and soldiers accompanied him. He stood in front of the long rows of prisoners and silently with a pointer in his gloved hand he indicated right, left, right, left. He did not have to say much. The *Kapos* and *Blockeltestes* knew what to do.

Sometimes the selections were done while we were dressed. Usually, this meant that Mengele would pick people to work in other labor camps or other parts of Auschwitz. But many times we were ordered to stand naked. Then Mengele chose the sickly looking people, the very skinny ones, and the ones with rashes or sores on their bodies. He checked our bodies quickly—a few red dots on the skin meant a death sentence. We knew that the order to undress meant that many of us would be torn from our families and friends forever.

The first time I stood naked was when I arrived in Auschwitz two months before. I felt helpless and degraded. But with time, I became numb to this humiliating procedure. There was no other way.

One day, while standing naked in line, Mengele touched me with his gloved hand. He moved my arm to see if I had a rash on my stomach. His touch was like my doctor's touch back home—gentle and kind. He had a faint smile on his lips. But his smile was the smile of death. My skin was clear. I was able to stay with my mother and sister.

Another week went by. There were more selections but we were still together. The constant fear of separation filled us with panic whenever the "Angel of Death" came to our camp.

One time he asked all the women who were twins to step forward. I looked at my mother, not knowing what to do. I was a twin. My twin brother had died at the age of two. My mother was also a twin and her brother had also died in infancy. Without saying a word to each other we did not move. Later we heard about Mengele's terrible medical experiments on twins.

Three months after our arrival in Auschwitz, during the last week of July 1944, the dreaded day came. Dr. Mengele visited us again. Mother, Lilly and I were holding on to each other. Mengele was looking for young women, sixteen to forty years old. I was sixteen years old, Lilly was twenty and Mother was forty-three.

The women prisoners were lined up: five to a row, a thousand women in a column. Each line stepped up to Mengele. He looked and pointed—right or left. Our line approached him. He pointed: Mother to the left, Lilly and I to the right. Because we had not been ordered to undress, we knew that the women selected would be sent to work at another camp.

My heart was pounding so fast I thought it would leap out of my body. What should we do? What will happen to Mother? We cannot leave her alone.

Lilly looked at me and then quickly stepped out of our line and into the other line, next to Mother. I waited a few minutes and when I thought no one was looking, also sneaked into the other line. Suddenly, someone grabbed me from behind, slapped me hard on the face, and pushed me back into the right line. I met the eyes of an SS officer. He pointed to his rifle. I knew what he meant: You better stay put. You will not get a second chance.

The selection ended. I was taken away. Mother and Lilly went back to their barracks. We waved and cried until we lost sight of each other.

I went through another *Entlousing*—sprayed from head to toe with a strong disinfectant. Then I was taken to another camp in Auschwitz to await a work assignment.

The next day I discovered that I was in the camp next to Mother and Lilly and I was able to see and talk to them every day. I stayed in this camp for two and a half months.

The conditions in my camp were the same as in the one before. The only difference was that our arms were tattooed with identification numbers.

Tattoo

Somehow, in all the misery of Auschwitz we always knew the dates and holidays of the year. Through the prisoners' grapevine we also heard news about the war but we were never sure if it was the truth, propaganda or just rumors.

I was lying on the bunk bed in my barracks thinking of the coming day—my birthday. I was alone, separated from my mother and sister. What will this day bring me? Maybe a miracle will happen and I will wake up at home and Auschwitz will be just a nightmare. I looked at my surroundings and I knew it was the other way around. I prayed for sleep and perhaps a comforting dream to escape the misery, if only for a few hours. But my nagging hunger brought me back to the horrible present. Finally, I fell into a fitful sleep.

The next morning we went through the usual routine—standing in line for the latrine and then standing for hours for *Appell*. The rest of the morning we just lingered around aimlessly with our constant hunger. There was no work to do to help pass the endless hours. Suddenly, we heard shouting. "Line up! Fast! Everybody move!"

As we ran to line up a strange thing happened. The *Blockelteste* stood in front of us and yelled, "Today you must line up in alphabetical order, according to last names. Quickly!" We all looked at each other in amazement.

"What is happening? We always use only our first names here. What does it matter what our last names are?" I asked the girl standing next to me.

No one knew what was going on. We could not talk as we had to rush and obey orders. The *Blockelteste* started to shout again, "Now we will go to the other side of the camp. Stay in alphabetical order. Move, quickly!"

A group of old-timer women were seated at tables waiting for us. I was standing far back in line and could not see what they were doing. As we approached the table we were asked our full name and country of origin. One of the women wrote it down and dictated a number to the other woman. She had an instrument in her hand that looked like a fountain pen with blue ink in it and an injection needle at the end. By the time I was close enough to see what was going on I realized what was happening—we were getting our arms tattooed. After a long wait my turn came up.

"What is your name and where are you from?" the first woman asked me.

"Edith Slomovits from Chust, Hungary which used to be Czechoslovakia before the war," I answered.

She wrote it down and dictated a number to the other girl. Then she grabbed my left arm and started to poke my skin with this strange instrument. With little needle stings the blue ink went under my skin as she tattooed on the inside of my arm: A-13215.

While this woman was working on my arm I was so overwhelmed with thoughts that I did not feel the pain. I am getting a number. From now on I will be A-13215. I will not be able to switch from one barracks to another. The Germans will have a permanent record of where I am and where I should be. They are de-humanizing me. I will not be a person any more, only a number. Now, I am marked just like cattle.

Then other thoughts overtook me. If the Germans bother to give me a tattoo number then they must have some plans for me—some *living* plans. Perhaps they will send me away to work—away from this hell called Auschwitz. I am not going to die here!

By the time my tattoo was done I did not feel humiliated at all. I felt hopeful. I will live! They branded me. They took away my family, my belongings, my hair. But they could not take away my will to live.

My arm healed in a few days and the number was there forever. It was August 18, 1944—my seventeenth birthday.

Sundays

Sundays in Auschwitz were different from the rest of the week. We stood *Appell* only once, in the morning. No selections were made on Sundays. These small changes from the usual routine made all the difference to us and we waited for Sunday all week long.

The meager meals were the same as always. After the morning *Appell* we milled around aimlessly outside or returned to our barracks and lay on our bunk beds.

In the late afternoon, after we devoured our daily rations, we remained outside. Thousands of us went to the fences to talk to relatives and friends on the other side. I went to the fence to talk to my mother and Lilly. We stood as close as possible to each other without touching the high voltage wires which could instantly electrocute us. We had to shout to be heard because the Sunday crowds on both sides of the fence were even larger than on weekdays. We thought it was safer to go to the fences on Sundays because there were fewer SS guards there than during the rest of the week.

The shouting, crying and pushing was unbearable. Thousands of women on both sides of the fence—like two human walls—tried to comfort and give hope to each other.

One day, while I was waiting for my mother and sister, I overheard a conversation between two girls standing on either side of the fence.

"Who is left from your family?" one girl asked.

"Just the two of us. Me and my good humor," the other girl answered with a sad smile.

Hearing this good-natured remark gave me the impetus to go on. I always wanted to hear and believe in the positive.

Suddenly, a shot rang out. We stood startled for a few seconds and then everyone ran away. As I ran I looked back but could not see what happened. Later, I heard that a woman was shot to death on our side of the fence. The prisoners talked about this incident for a few days but the next Sunday we were all at the fence again.

Again, we talked and shouted to each other and again, without warning, a shot rang out. Another young woman was killed. Everyone standing around the fallen woman ran away. I looked around to find out where the shot came from but I did not see any SS guards. Then I looked up and saw an SS soldier in the guard tower aiming his rifle at us.

This random killing of a prisoner was repeated every Sunday. I knew it was the doing of that same SS guard in the tower, entertaining himself on a Sunday afternoon.

One Sunday, in early September of 1944, I was standing at the fence talking to my mother and Lilly. Standing next to me was Gitta Salamon, Lilly's friend, who was also talking to her mother on the other side. All of a sudden, I heard a high-pitched sound. It was so close, so loud, that for a moment I thought *I* had been shot. I jumped back and then I saw Gitta lying on the ground. I felt as if I was meant to be the target that Sunday because I was much closer to the fence than she was. Gitta was killed while her mother looked on. I ran away as fast as I could. I never stood so close to the fence again.

The picture of Gitta lying on the ground and her mother fainting on the other side has never left me.

My Last Day In Auschwitz

The morning *Appell* was over. We were standing outside the barracks when I heard someone yelling, "Mengele is coming!"

"What does he want today?" we asked each other. "What will his selections be for this time?"

"Line up! Fast!" the shouting began. We ran to line up—thousands of women in single file—ready for Mengele's inspection.

Mengele reached our group with his assistant officers and the *Blockelteste*. As always, he wore his immaculate white gloves and carried a small pointer in his hand. Everyone was silent as he pointed right and left. Healthy, strong women to the right. Weak, sickly women to the left.

Right and left, right and left went the pointer. We stood in our designated groups for a long time until Mengele left our camp. Then all the women on the left side returned to the barracks.

The four hundred women selected for the right side, including myself, remained standing outside. Seeing the healthier looking women around me, I knew we would be sent to work somewhere. I prayed we would leave Auschwitz. Even though I did not know what was going on in the outside world or in other concentration camps, I believed that any place must be better than Auschwitz.

How was I going to reach my mother and sister and let them know that I was picked to go away? There was no possibility of reaching them because we were ordered to leave immediately.

"This group, let's go! Fast! March!" the *Blockelteste* yelled.

We were taken to the *Entlausing* building where we were given our second cold shower since our arrival in May, five months before. We were sprayed with disinfectant powder and received different clothing; one pair of underwear, one dress and a coat. What a treat this coat was. It was also another sign that we were going away to work.

Dressed in our "new" clothes, our march to the train began—a train that would bring us to a new destination, hopefully a better one. We left our camp and reached the main road of Auschwitz—the same road that brought us here a few months ago.

The remaining prisoners stood by the fences watching us leave. As we marched, I searched their faces hoping to see someone who knew my mother and sister so that I could send a message to them letting them know that I had left Auschwitz. But we had to march quickly and there was no time for any communication with these prisoners.

Suddenly, from the corner of my eye, I saw someone running alongside of me on the other side of the fence. It was a little woman trying hard to keep up with us. I looked again and recognized my mother. It was a miracle seeing my mother at this crucial moment. We tried to talk to each other quickly.

"Mother, where is Lilly?" I shouted.

"She left Auschwitz yesterday," my mother answered.

"Where did she go?"

"I don't know. Mengele was here and he selected a group of young women. I hope she left for a work camp."

I was marching, my mother was running. We tried to say goodbye. We tried to promise each other that our family would reunite one day, but we could not. We were choking with tears. I looked back at my mother as long as I could, not knowing when I would ever see her again. We reached the gate—a last wave, a last kiss in the air—and we were separated from each other.

We were outside the camp on the main road. A long cattle train waited for us. We stopped and waited for the order to board. I turned around to look at Auschwitz for the last time when I heard a voice calling. I did not see anyone. I did not know where the sound was coming from.

"Help me! Help me!" the voice became louder.

Then I saw a small face peering out of the cellar window of a large, concrete building. The window had iron bars on it and inside the cellar hundreds of women were locked up like animals in a cage. I moved closer to the window and saw a young girl, my age, crying and asking for help. I tried to talk to the girl but did not know what to say. There was nothing I or anyone else could do. I knew that these women in the cellar would never get out. Their fate was the gas chamber.

Many hours had passed since we left Camp B. We were exhausted, still waiting for permission to sit down. We were counted over and over again by the old-timers and the SS.

Additional SS officers arrived and started talking to the *Blockelteste* and *Kapos* in charge of our group. The talking turned into an argument. We did not hear what they were saying but we could see the *Blockelteste* gesturing angrily and not giving in to whatever it was that the SS wanted. The arguing went on for a long time. Finally, we were told to board the train.

It was completely dark inside the cattle car. We sat on the bare floor but the train did not move. We waited for several more hours. One of the old-timers came into our car and told us what happened.

The SS officers in charge of the gas chambers had extra room for a few hundred more women. When they saw our group standing in line for the train they wanted to take us to fill up the gas chambers. Luckily, the *Blockelteste* and her helpers did not give in to their demands. They argued with the SS telling them that our group was destined for a factory in Germany. They knew that if they did not deliver the specified number of women they would have to pay with their own lives. This time our lives were saved by these old-timers.

All of a sudden, the camp sirens sounded and we heard explosions—one after another. We thought the Americans were bombing Auschwitz. I was very scared but after our narrow escape from the gas chambers I believed that the bombing would not harm us. Then it was quiet.

After several more hours of waiting, the train began to move. We left Auschwitz!

◆

After the war I heard that on the night of October 7, 1944, the night I left Auschwitz, the explosions I heard were not from American bombers. That night, there was a prisoner revolt in Auschwitz. Over the course of several months, a group of male prisoners managed to smuggle in explosives from the munitions factory where they worked. Secretly, they had built bombs and planned the revolt. On that night they destroyed two crematoriums and killed several SS guards. Some of the prisoners escaped. Those who were caught were killed but their bravery slowed down the monstrous German killing machine.

Sabotage

We left Auschwitz in October 1944 and were transferred to the village of Taucha, near Leipzig, Germany. In Taucha there was a small labor camp of about 1,200 people from all over Europe. The conditions in Taucha were much better than in Auschwitz—any camp was better than Auschwitz—and we felt lucky to have been sent there.

The barracks were smaller—thirty people per room. Each prisoner had their own bed, blanket and straw to sleep on.

The food was better and we received a bit more. We were fed twice daily. At noon we got a bowl of vegetable soup with little pieces of meat in it. The evening meal consisted of two slices of bread, one slice of salami and a small square of margarine. But we were still hungry all the time.

A male prisoner twice my size received the same amount of food as me. When I saw how hungry the men were I thought of my father and brother. Are they so hungry too? Are they so miserable? If they were only here with me I would try to help them. The only "good" that came from the separation of my family was that we did not have to see each other suffering.

There was a large weapons factory an hour's walk from the camp where we worked around the clock in twelve hour shifts. We went to work at either 5:00 a.m. or 5:00 p.m. It was always dark no matter when we started. Our shifts were alternated every week.

We marched to the factory in a long column, five people to a row. Not too many SS guards watched us. It would have been easy to step out of line and disappear. It crossed my mind every day. But where would I go? If I managed to escape to the village or to the countryside I would be instantly recognized by my odd clothing and shaved head. No German would have helped me. An escape would have been sure suicide.

It was much better to work on the day shift. That shift slept at night and received two meals during the working hours. The night shift prisoners had to work for twelve hours without getting any meals. They returned to camp at 6:00 a.m. tired and hungry and went straight to sleep. At noon they were awakened to receive their mid-day soup. After this meal they went back to sleep and had to get up again at 4:00 p.m. to wash, get their evening meal and go to work. As hungry as they were, they tried to save some bread for the long, twelve hour stretch at night.

The factory manufactured the *Panzer Faust*—an anti-tank missile. I worked on the welding machines. Each machine had a thin metal rod protruding from its side. Two girls sat on either side of the rod. On the rod we fit a pipe onto which we welded a small metal plate. In order to weld the plate to the pipe we had to push a foot pedal eleven times, simultaneously adjusting the pipe with both hands. Both the pipe and the plate had three holes. We had to match the holes exactly. If they mismatched even a fraction of a millimeter, the pipe was useless. It had to be taken to another department where it was dismantled and reassembled.

The unwelded pipes were stacked at the side of the machine. One of the male prisoner's job was to supply the workers at the machine with the metal plates. Each time he gave us fifty plates he made a chalk mark on the side of the machine.

In the beginning, each team of girls made approximately 600 pieces a day. The German foreman pushed for more and the girls strained harder and harder. After several weeks each team was producing 1,000 units in a twelve hour shift. But the SS wanted even more. They promised us a bonus—extra food—for the girls who produced the most units. Many girls overexerted themselves, desperately trying to earn the extra food. By the end of the second month many girls were making 1,500 units a day and this became the norm. I was not one of these girls.

One day, I watched the male prisoner marking the machines to indicate how many units were being made. Secretly, I got hold of a piece of chalk and added some marks of my own whenever he was not looking. Many times, even my partner did not know what I was doing. Using this secret method I added 300-400 non-existent units per day. By the time the work shift ended I felt elated that I had "produced" about 800 units. Every time I added a chalk mark I felt I was shortening the war and fighting the Nazis.

Once, during the night shift, I almost fell asleep at the machine. I sensed the German foreman staring at me and I started to work faster.

"I don't like the way you work," he said to me. "You do not produce as much as the other girls."

I felt the blood draining from my face as I looked up at him. What is he going to do to me? He looked at me—a small, skinny, terrified girl—for a long time.

"From now on I will keep you on the day shift but you

must produce 1,000 units per day," he said sternly. "If not, I will report you to the SS."

I could not believe my ears. I will be one of the lucky ones who works on the day shift all the time. I will be able to sleep all night, have my food during the waking hours and will not have to save any bread for the night. This was the best thing that could happen to me at the time.

"Thank you, thank you! I promise I will work better," I answered quickly before he could change his mind.

After several days on the day shift, I resumed my secret method and added chalk marks to "increase" my production.

For several weeks my partner at the machine was a girl from Budapest. As we worked, we played a game to help pass the time. We fantasized that after the war we will visit each other and we imagined what food we would serve in our homes. She would serve me delicious Hungarian dishes—chicken *paprikash*, veal *goulash*, and for dessert a rich, chocolate *torte*. I would make her a traditional Sabbath meal of *gefilte* fish, chicken soup, *kugel*, chopped liver, *cholent* and *tzimes*. We went on and on with all the dishes we remembered from home. The game did not make us less hungry but it gave us hope.

When I watched the girls straining to produce the maximum amount of units I tried to talk to them.

"What are you doing? Why are you pushing yourselves to make more and more? Do you realize that you push that foot pedal 16,500 times a day? Don't you see that you are making more ammunition for the Germans and this will only prolong the war? Don't you want to go home?"

They looked at me with sad eyes, turned away and did not answer. They were afraid. The bonus, the extra food that was promised to them, blinded them to everything else.

When I realized that I could not convince them and that I could only act alone, I started sabotaging in another way. Cautiously, I mismatched the holes of the metal plate with the holes of the pipe.

But, there were times when I had misgivings. The bonus was given out. It was a whole herring and I did not get one, for I was known as a poor worker. For a moment I thought, "Maybe I was wrong. I could have had a herring." But then I found my answer. For one herring should I prolong the war? No! I did the right thing. As it turned out, there was never another bonus given out.

One day an officer from the *Wermacht*, (the German Army) who was an expert on the *Panzer Faust*, came to inspect our factory. A good missile could destroy a tank but one with even the smallest defect would miss the target. The officer spoke to the German foreman.

"Who is sabotaging in this factory?" he shouted. "Many of the *Panzer Fausts* are not performing. They explode before they reach the target. Many go off target completely!"

He went on and on. My heart pounded wildly. I wanted to shout out, "I am doing it! I am fighting the Nazis!" But I continued to work quietly.

When a pipe was ready, it was put on a conveyor belt and sent to the next department. Once on the conveyor belt there was no way of knowing who made it. The *Wermacht* officer was standing at the head of the conveyor belt, checking every pipe. When he saw that it was impossible to detect who was sabotaging, he came up with an idea. He ordered a little device to be put on every machine that numbered each pipe before it went on the conveyor belt. The new system scared me. I would not be able to sabotage by mismatching any more. I could still make fewer pieces, but would no longer be able to make defective ones and I would have to be extremely careful.

One day, the German foreman told us, without much explanation, that the numbering devices did not work. They were taken off the machines. From that day on until our evacuation from the camp, I made more bad pipes than good ones.

◆

I resisted the Nazis and I was not alone. Whether it was intentional sabotage or quiet suffering, it was resistance. Not giving into the hunger and the cold, not breaking down from the grueling work, enduring every imaginable pain, anguish and torture—that was resistance. Every one of us who survived— resisted.

The Gypsies

In Taucha there were several groups of prisoners. The largest group was from Hungary—eight hundred Jewish men and women. There were also about two hundred non-Jewish women who were political dissidents or criminals transferred to Taucha from other prisons. There was another group of two hundred young Gypsy women from all over Europe.

The Gypsies, regardless of their country of origin, had a common language, Romany. Most of them were from wandering tribes who traveled in wagons from town to town making a living from fortune telling, cleaning outhouses, and petty thefts. The other Gypsies were from the big cities; Berlin, Prague, Budapest and Bucharest. They were professional dancers, singers, acrobats and musicians. They were more sophisticated than the others.

The Gypsy women were transferred to Taucha at the same time that we were, but they were the only ones who arrived wearing striped prisoners' clothing. The rest of their families were left behind in Auschwitz never to be seen again.

As in Auschwitz, men, women and Gypsies lived in separate camps. But unlike Auschwitz, the barbed wire that separated the camps in Taucha was not electrically charged.

At the factory, we all worked together and could talk to one another. When I first met the Gypsies I was friendly to them and we exchanged information about ourselves.

Some of the male prisoners had contact with German officers and civilians when they did extra work for them. In exchange, they received cigarettes.

Many of the Gypsy women traded their bread for cigarettes. After the women finished smoking their precious cigarettes they were still hungry. With nothing left to trade but their bodies, they slept with the male prisoners for a piece of bread. This was very risky, for prisoners caught together were immediately sent to a death camp.

A few days before New Year's Eve of 1945, I was surprised to hear from my fellow prisoners that there would be a performance put on for us in the camp. The SS ordered the Gypsies to prepare a show. The excitement was great. It seemed unbelievable. We had already forgotten about such things as shows and entertainment.

On the day of the performance, we were taken to the dining area. All the women prisoners sat on the ground. The Gypsy girls danced, sang and did acrobatics. They made us forget, for a little while, where we were. I was so grateful to them that afterwards I went up to the performers and thanked them.

I particularly remember a beautiful young Gypsy girl from Berlin. She was tall with straight, black hair, large, dark eyes and a charming smile. Somehow, she obtained a top hat and a cane. She entertained us with a lively singing and tap dance act. She was full of energy and I could have watched her dance for hours. But after the show, life went back to the same bleak routine.

Several weeks after the performance one of the older Gypsy women at the factory pushed me roughly for no reason.

"Why did you push me?" I asked her. "What did I do to you?"

"You dirty Jew!" she yelled at me. "Because of *you* I am here in this camp."

"Because of me?" I asked, surprised by her response. "I am as miserable here as you are. Why is it my fault?"

"Because you Jews caused the war and because of the war I am here!" she screamed.

By this time, a big crowd had gathered around us. The Jewish prisoners looked on in silent shock as the Gypsies and other non-Jewish prisoners joined in the yelling.

"I did not cause the war, Hitler did," I said.

"No, Hitler said that the Jews made the war and he was right. Everything is your fault."

I tried to reason with her but it was impossible. I walked away crying. I did not understand how I, a seventeen year old girl, could have caused this terrible war.

From that day on, I kept my distance from the Gypsies.

The Gray Woolen Socks

Early one morning in the infirmary at Taucha, I woke up and looked out the window. It was snowing and bitter cold outside. In the infirmary it was dark and quiet. I could see figures rushing in and out of one of the small barracks where the toilets and cold water faucets were. The prisoners were getting ready to go to work. As the darkness started to fade I recognized many of their tired faces.

For the moment, I felt secure in the warm room where I had been for the past three weeks. But I knew that in another day or two I would be sent back to work.

It is hard to believe that there was an infirmary in a labor camp, but the Nazis needed us in relatively good condition so that we could work in their munitions factory. The infirmary consisted of a large room with a small entry hall. There were two rows of beds and a little stove in the middle of the room for heating. The only medical instrument in the infirmary was a thermometer.

A young Ukrainian prisoner named Maria served as our nurse. She was anti-Semitic and showed favoritism to her own people. She made sure that there were always more non-Jewish women in the infirmary than Jewish ones even though we outnumbered them two to one. She enforced strict discipline and never hesitated to strike the prisoners in her care. She had the power to help or harm us. I was terrified of Maria.

The camp had one doctor, a Hungarian Jew, for all 1,200 prisoners. He showed compassion for every person and his kindness gave much support to the sick.

There was a small room in the infirmary where the doctor examined the prisoners. If the thermometer indicated fever and the doctor could determine an illness which required rest, he sent the prisoner to the infirmary. But, to report sick was very risky as the Germans often sent the sick back to Auschwitz or other death camps. When someone was sent away we never saw them again.

December arrived and the days became colder. My large, mismatched men's shoes were worn out. I had no socks. I did not even have rags to wrap around my feet to keep the snow out of my shoes. I developed a cough and every evening I felt feverish and extremely tired. My friends urged me to see the doctor but I was afraid. I was not getting better. Finally, I summoned up my courage and went to see him.

"You have a fever, my child, but it may go away," he told me as he listened to my lungs. "Try to stay indoors as much as possible and if you do not feel better in a few days come see me again."

"But, *Herr* Doctor, you won't send me away from Taucha, will you?" I asked.

"No, no. I will not let them send you away," he reassured me.

I went back to work but my condition worsened. My fever went up and I felt pain in my left shoulder. I went back to the doctor and he told me that the top of my left lung was infected. He sent me to the infirmary. I was so relieved not to have to return to work in this cold weather that I forgot about the possible risk of being in the infirmary. What a luxury it was to stay in bed, in a warm room, and not have to get up at 4:30 in the morning.

In the infirmary, the nights were quiet and the days started late. But our two daily meals were not different from those of the working prisoners.

Our temperature was measured daily. When patients recovered they were released and others took their place. When patients died they were taken to other camps, as Taucha had no crematorium.

After a few days of rest I started to walk around the room. All twenty beds were occupied by women of different ages and nationalities. Several languages were spoken—Yiddish, Hungarian, Polish, Czech, French, Russian, and Romany—but broken German was our common language.

Every day, a bedridden French woman in her early forties asked me to toast her bread on top of the little stove.

"Very dark, almost burnt," she told me.

I gladly did it for her, and one day she surprised me by giving me a piece of toast for my help.

In the bed next to mine was a Jewish girl in her twenties.

"What is your name?" I asked her in Yiddish.

"Zlate," she told me. We used only first names.

"Why are you here?" I asked her.

"I have syphilis," she answered simply.

"Syphilis?!" I was shocked. Even though I was young, I knew the seriousness of that disease. I had never heard of a Jewish girl getting syphilis. "How did you get it?"

"It happened before I was taken to concentration camp," she told me. "I had an affair with a man I hardly knew."

"Why did you do it?" I asked.

"He told me he would marry me," she said quietly.

"And...," I pressed her for more.

"I never saw him again." She fell silent and turned away from me. We never spoke about it again. I left the infirmary before Zlate did and never found out what happened to her.

Across from my bed were two Polish women in their early fifties. All day long they chattered loudly in Polish, punctuating every sentence with *Prosze Pani* (dear lady). I had to restrain myself from shouting, "Shut up! Stop! Enough already!"

In another bed was a young Gypsy girl. She suffered from advanced tuberculosis. She died and was taken away.

The next day her bed was occupied by a pretty, twenty-eight year old woman from Hungary named Vera. She came in with a fever and an abscess on her leg. She was in great pain. The doctor took one look at her leg and said, "Vera, dear, this does not look good. I must operate immediately to save your life. As you know, I have no instruments, no anesthesia and no medication."

The room was silent, filled with tension. An operation, here? How is it possible?

"I have a pocket knife. I can hypnotize you so that you will feel no pain," he said. "If you agree, I will try this operation."

"Yes, yes *Herr* Doctor," Vera said. "I agree to everything. I want to live!"

The doctor placed the pocket knife in the stove to sterilize it. He tied a string around a small stone to make a pendulum and swung it back and forth in front of Vera's eyes. The hypnosis began. We all held our breath, watching and praying. Slowly, Vera closed her eyes. The doctor started to operate with the little knife. She was very quiet, moaning softly in her sleep. Some of us tore up our undershirts and made bandages for her. When the surgery was over the doctor bandaged her leg and woke her up. She felt much better and did not remember anything. Vera recuperated completely and was sent back to work.

One evening, Maria went out to meet one of her friends

returning from work. We could hear them talking in the hall-way. A few minutes later Maria returned to the main room of the infirmary.

I got up to get a drink of water and wandered into the little hallway. There, on a bench, I saw a pair of new gray woolen knee socks. I knew that in a few days I would be discharged from the infirmary and sent back to work in the cold. I had no socks and here I stood, with nobody around, looking at a pair of socks as if they were waiting for me. Should I take them? Who did they belong to? I hesitated, but I knew that if I did not take them, the next person coming by would. I needed the socks desperately. I do not know if I stood there for thirty seconds or thirty minutes but finally I took the socks, hid them under my dress and went back to bed. Once inside, I carefully tucked the socks under my mattress and did not tell anyone.

Maria went out again but suddenly she burst back into the room yelling, "I had a pair of woolen knee socks outside. Who took them?" No one answered. "I'm going to search everyone and God help the person who took them," she screamed.

I was so scared I did not know what to do. I would have given them back but I knew that even if I returned the socks voluntarily, Maria would beat me. I lay in bed praying silently.

Maria continued screaming and then abruptly left the room. There was not a sound in the infirmary or the hallway. After a few seconds she returned. She was holding a pair of gray woolen knee socks.

"I found my socks," she said simply and the matter was closed.

I looked at her socks. They were identical to the pair I had found. When the lights went out, I checked under my mattress and my socks were still there. But how did Maria get the other pair? There was no one in the hallway when she went out the second time and no one had come in. Maria had her socks and I had mine.

Two days later I was discharged from the infirmary. I put

on my new socks and went back to work. The socks kept my feet warm and dry and I wore them all winter until the end of the war.

◆

The mystery of the socks puzzles me to this day. The only answer I have is that God provided this personal miracle for me.

Rachel's Siddur

She must have felt my stare. She lifted her eyes from the *Siddur*, looked at me, but did not interrupt her prayers. When she finished she came over to me.

"Would you like to say the **Shmah?" she asked me quietly.

"Yes, please," I said.

"What is your name?" she asked me.

"Edith, what is yours?"

"Rachel," she said in a friendly voice and handed me her cherished *Siddur*.

I took it in disbelief. A *Siddur* in my hands, in this place! I started to say the prayers. I was afraid someone would take the

*A Jewish Prayer Book
**A Jewish prayer stating that God is One

Siddur away, or worse yet, I would wake up from a dream.

Rachel watched me with a reassuring look. "It's all right. Don't worry. Say your prayers."

I kissed the *Siddur* and handed it back to Rachel. I wanted to thank her but she put her finger to her lips and nodded no.

"Don't thank me, Edith. We all pray for the same things."

"How did you...where did you get this *Siddur*?" I asked in amazement.

"I have it for some time now," she answered evasively. "Whenever you want to pray, just come to me."

Later, I found out that she had "organized" this Siddur in Auschwitz, (before we were transported to Taucha) by trading several of her daily portions of bread.

"My God," I thought. "How strong she must be to give up her bread." Bread meant life for every prisoner.

I saw Rachel whenever we were on the same work shift at the munitions factory. The *Siddur* was always with her and she let me pray from it whenever I wanted. I wished I could do something for her too.

One day, I saw Rachel carrying a big sack and her *Siddur*. We talked for a while. She gave me her *Siddur* and I prayed silently. I asked her if there was anything I could do for her. She smiled and again evaded my question.

"Did you know that last week was Purim?" Rachel asked.

"Yes," I answered, "and Passover is coming soon."

We were silent, each with our own thoughts—perhaps the same thoughts; Passover, the family, the *Seder*...

"What do you think, Rachel, will we be home for Passover?"

"How I wish that were so but it does not seem like it," she answered.

"But the news is good. Maybe the war will end by then," I persisted.

"Yes, the news is good, but what do we really know? Only God knows the answer," she replied.

"God took the Jews out of Egypt, couldn't He take us out of here? Why are we here in the first place? Where is God?" I pleaded.

"God is here," she said with quiet conviction. "You must not lose hope."

Suddenly, I had a revelation. I forgot about everyone around me. I felt as if I was standing before God alone, just God and I. I realized that the answer was there from my very first day in Auschwitz. I blamed the Germans, not God, for my being in concentration camp, for being separated from my family, for being so very hungry, cold and miserable. Once I understood this, I prayed to God to help me out of this situation.

I looked back at Rachel's large and heavy bag and again asked her what was in it. She told me that she was exchanging some of her daily bread rations for carrots, squash and other vegetables so she would not have to eat bread during the eight days of Passover.

"How do you make exchanges?" I asked her.

"It's not easy. It takes time and patience so I started early," she said.

Then I knew what I could do for her. I asked around and did some *organizieren* for her and myself.

Passover arrived. A group of girls who did not have to go to the night shift sat together in the barracks and had a *Seder*. Rachel read some passages from her *Siddur*. Some of the Passover blessings we knew by heart. We did not sing. We meditated in silence. When we came to the last sentence of the *Haggadah we repeated over and over again: "Next year in Jerusalem…Next year in Jerusalem…" *Whenever* we will be liberated will be our next year. *Wherever* we will be liberated will be our Jerusalem.

That night none of us ate bread. I did not touch bread for the next twenty four hours. Rachel stayed away from bread for the entire eight days of Passover.

---

*The book containing the Passover Seder service

◆

Five weeks after Passover we were liberated. I heard from a former camp inmate that Rachel survived and returned to her native Romania. She married a *Chassid*, had several children and lived a religious life.

*An ultra-Orthodox Jew

March to Freedom

It was April of 1945. I had been in Auschwitz and Taucha for a year.

Something was different. A strange tension hung in the air. The night shift workers had returned but the next shift, my shift, was not sent out to the factory. We stood outside our barracks along with the night shift people, waiting for the next order.

The SS guards were running around frantically. We knew the Germans were losing the war and the end was near, but we did not know when, where, and how it would end. Every day seemed like an eternity. We looked at each other with questioning eyes but no one had any answers.

Suddenly, the SS started to shout *"Raus, schnell, Appell!"* We lined up—five people to a row. We had no belongings but some of us managed to run back into the barracks and grab a blanket from our bunks. We had no idea where we were going. We prayed that we would not be taken to another concentration camp.

The SS did not bother to count us, as they used to do so meticulously. They took up position and with their rifles pointed at us, we evacuated the camp. The march began.

The first day we marched twenty-five miles without getting any food. The spring rain fell continuously. At nightfall, when we reached a forest—hungry, exhausted and wet—we were allowed to sit and rest.

At dawn, before the Germans had a chance to line us up, we saw Allied planes fill the sky. The Germans panicked. They pushed us deeper into the forest and ordered us to lay flat on the ground. Somehow, I managed to crawl out into a clearing and watch the planes. Bombs were falling. I heard explosions all around me but I was not afraid. I believed the Allies would never hurt me. I was not the enemy.

When the bombing stopped, our march continued. The road became wider and more populated. There were three columns of people moving steadily.

We, the prisoners, were the first row. We were dressed shabbily, many of us without shoes, some of us with blankets thrown over our heads. The blankets were soaking wet but it was better with than without them.

Moving along next to us, in wagons and on foot, were a few scattered units of the German army—what was left of it.

In the third column were the German civilians, fleeing their homes before the approaching Russian army. Seeing the German army and the civilians running away gave me new strength to go on.

I felt even more optimistic when I read the writing on the village walls. *"Wir werden nicht kapitulieren!"* "We will not surrender!" The mere fact that the Germans used the word "surrender" was proof to me that they considered that a possibility. What a difference this was from Hitler's earlier diatribes when he boasted about his military triumphs and his plans to conquer Europe and destroy the Jewish people. Over and over again, in every village, I saw *"Wir werden nicht kapitulieren!"*

"The war will be over soon," I thought. "I will go home to my family. I will hug them and kiss them. I will eat bread and more bread and then some more. But right now I am still in the Germans' hands and I must do everything possible to survive."

Many of the girls marching next to me did not have blankets. They were cold and miserable. The German wagons filled with soldiers, blankets and other supplies rolled by. I looked around making sure no one was watching and grabbed a blanket off of a moving wagon. I gave it to one of the girls in my row. I waited, nothing happened. I snatched another blanket off the next wagon and gave it to another girl. The German soldiers paid no attention to me. They were too busy with their own troubles. Gradually, I supplied myself and the girls around me with dry military blankets.

We marched twenty to twenty-five miles a day. I was exhausted and could barely walk when a new idea came to me. I jumped onto the back of a wagon and rode on it for a few miles.

"Edith, what are you doing? Come back here!" the girls shouted when they saw me riding on the wagon.

"Don't worry," I told them. "I'll wait for you."

"The SS will shoot you. Don't do it!"

"They won't notice me," I assured them.

I rode this way for a while and then hopped off the wagon and waited for my row of girls to catch up with me. When they arrived, I continued to walk with them. After a short while I got on another wagon and rode a few more miles. It was very dangerous, but I conserved a lot of energy this way—energy that helped me survive.

We passed many village signs. The names were unfamiliar to me. But after several days I started recognizing some of the names and realized that we were walking in a circle. The Germans were retreating, but whenever they thought they had reached a safe place it was already occupied by the Allies.

We reached the Dresden area after marching in a circle for over two weeks—a circle that was becoming smaller and smaller each day. I knew this meant the war would end soon.

One day, we arrived in a village we had been to before. The villagers were running around in confusion.

Suddenly, I saw a familiar face. It was Magda Horvat, a Gentile girl from my hometown. We had been classmates for four years.

Our eyes met but she did not recognize me. I was very skinny and dirty. My clothes were tattered. A wet blanket covered my head. I looked at her for a long time not knowing what to do.

"She is here in Germany," I thought. "She had to run away from Chust. She was afraid of the Russians."

I wanted to ask her for some food, but in spite of my painful hunger, my pride would not let me. I did not want her to see me in my condition.

As I looked at her I remembered the streets of Chust and how she had pretended not to recognize me because I was Jewish. I remembered how her parents took away my uncle's business and how her family moved into my grandparents' house.

When we were deported, she and other non-Jewish classmates of mine were at the train station. They were seated behind a long table checking our papers before we were forced to go through a humiliating body search. As they shoved us into the trains, Magda and her friends were laughing, not showing the slightest compassion for what was happening before their eyes.

As I looked at her, memories of my family filled my mind—memories and questions. Where is my father? My mother? My sister? My brother? Are they alive? Are they free already? Are they as hungry as I am? But shouts from the SS guards to move on brought me back to reality and without looking back at her I continued the march.

The next day, we arrived at a forest and stayed there for six days, until the end of the war. There was nowhere else to go. The Allies were closing in from all directions.

Finally, we were allowed to sit down after days of walking. The rest did not last long, however, as our hunger overtook everything else. During the march we were given only one piece of bread every three or four days. Some people lay on the wet ground, too weak to move on. Others looked around to see if there was anything they could do to stay alive.

One day, I saw a group of prisoners crowd around something. I went to see what it was but could not get close enough. Everyone was pushing and shouting. I started to push also and when I got to the center of the crowd I saw a dead horse laying on the ground. The prisoners were tearing off pieces of the carcass and eating it raw. Some prisoners used a piece of broken glass or a sharp rock. Others ripped off the flesh with their bare hands. Someone offered me his makeshift knife but I could not bring myself to eat from the dead horse.

As I wandered around the forest looking for something to eat I heard a faint trickling sound and followed it through the woods and down a hill. There, I saw a long forgotten sight—a small stream of clean, fresh water. The rain had stopped for a few hours and the sun came out.

The first thing I did was take a long drink. It was so refreshing, so clean, so pure—like a taste of freedom. I took off my dress and shoes and waded into the stream. There were several other girls there too. We washed ourselves, we drank the fresh water and for the first time in a long time, we laughed.

We felt new strength and courage returning to us.

"If there is such a beautiful stream of fresh water," I thought, "surely there must be other beautiful things in the world waiting for me." I was so excited I ran back to my group of girls to tell them about the stream.

"What happened to you?" they asked when I returned. "You look so clean, so happy, so different. What did you do? Where did you go?"

"I washed myself. I drank fresh, clean water, *Mayim Chayim*—life giving water. Beyond the hill is a beautiful stream of the most delicious water in the world. Go down there, all of you. Have a drink and wash yourselves," I told them. But only one girl, Irene, had the strength to get up and join me. The others were too weak to move.

Back in the forest, many of the SS troops were running away from the approaching Allies. Some stayed, hoping the prisoners would not turn against them.

The SS Commandant of the women's camp at Taucha had always called us swine, vermin, lice—never human beings with names. But now, in the final stage of the war, she suddenly remembered our names and approached us.

"Joli, will you tell the Russians that I was good to you?" she asked.

"Yes, of course," Joli answered.

"Agi, will you tell them that I never hit you? Will you say that I gave you enough food?"

"Yes, yes I will," she answered.

It was hard to believe that these Germans were asking for mercy from the very people they had tortured and abused. But they still had their guns, our fate was still in their hands and we were still afraid.

Another two days passed without receiving any food. The hunger was so unbearable that some of the prisoners sneaked into the villages to beg for food.

One day, three sisters slipped into the nearest village. Each sister went to a different house to ask for food. Before dark only two of the sisters returned to the forest. The third did not return. She disappeared without a trace.

The next day two other sisters tried their luck in the same village. But before they reached the village they were shot at by the SS. Somehow, they managed to get back to the forest. Both of them were bleeding heavily.

There was a Jewish doctor in our group—a prisoner like the rest of us. We rushed to get him but there was little he could do. He had no bandages or medication. The older sister survived but the younger one bled to death as we looked on helplessly.

Another day passed and the hunger did not subside. In spite of the other girls' tragedy I decided to go into the village and find some food. I asked the girls if anyone would join me but no one responded. They were afraid and warned me not to go, but my hunger overpowered all reasoning.

"Maybe it will be easier to die from a bullet than from hunger," I said. My mind was made up. Just as I said goodbye, Irene stood up.

"Wait Edith, I'll go with you," she said.

We arrived at the village and knocked on the door of the first farmhouse we saw. A woman answered and asked us what we wanted.

"Please, do you have any food for us? We are very hungry," I said.

"No, I don't have any," she answered and closed the door in our faces.

We tried at the next house and got the same response. It went on like this for some time. Irene wanted to quit and go back but I did not give up.

Finally, at the tenth house, a young girl opened the door. In the corner of the room, on the floor, I saw a small bowl with food in it.

"Please, a little food, a piece of bread, anything," I begged.

She shook her head no and started to close the door.

"What about the food in the corner?" I asked quickly before she could shut the door. She looked at us, surprised.

"That's the dog's food."

"May we have it?"

She shrugged her shoulders and gave it to us. We took the bowl feeling very fortunate. We ate every bit of it but we were still hungry.

We continued our search for food. It was raining and we found ourselves further and further from the forest. We realized that we would not reach our group in the forest before dark and decided to look for a place to stay. We asked at every farmhouse, but again, the answer was always "no."

Just as the situation seemed hopeless, one of the villagers told us we could stay in his barn in a small laundry room next to the pig sty. It was an empty room with a large kettle of hot water in it.

We washed ourselves and our clothes in the hot water—a luxury we had not felt since we were taken away from our homes a year ago. We smiled at each other with new hope.

In the morning a noise outside woke us up. We looked out the little window and saw German soldiers—their wagons, cars and horses—running around in panic. We saw the officers tearing the Nazi insignia off their uniforms. Others hastily changed from their uniforms into civilian clothes taken from the villagers. They were afraid they would be caught by the Allies.

A group of French prisoners of war were working for the Germans. One of the French prisoners entered our room and was surprised to see us there. Despite our broken German we managed to explain who we were and how hungry we were. He left and a half hour later returned with a five pound loaf of bread and a package of margarine. He also brought us straw so that we would not have to sleep on the bare concrete floor. He told us that a German officer asked him to fix his car and his price had been this bread and margarine.

We could not thank him enough and looked at the large bread in disbelief. We did not dare eat it all as we did not know when the war would end and how long the bread would have to last us.

We felt very lucky. We had bread, margarine, a roof over our heads, straw to sleep on, hot water and no SS troops around. We stayed inside the room not wanting to risk our lives anymore. We were still prisoners but now we were prisoners in hiding.

Avremele

The next morning we woke up at daybreak. There was a suspicious stillness outside. We looked out the window. The German soldiers, their cars, wagons and horses were all gone. The villagers were in their homes, their windows and doors shuttered close.

The sun came out. It was a beautiful morning. We watched and waited.

Slowly, new sounds reached us—sounds of cars, tanks and people approaching. In the distance I saw soldiers, but they were not German soldiers—they were Russians.

"The war is over!" I shouted. Irene and I hugged one another and cried. We were free!

I took a few tentative steps into the courtyard and found myself facing a tall, burly, Russian officer. He was six feet tall. No, ten feet tall. Maybe a hundred feet tall in my eyes. We stared at each other for a long time, too startled to speak. My mind worked fast. I knew Czech and a few words of Russian.

"*Ya jestem Evrejka,*" I am a Jew, I said.

"*Evrejka? Du bist a Yid?*" You are a Jew? He was surprised. "*Du redst Yiddish?*" Do you speak Yiddish, he asked.

I nodded yes.

"I am also a Jew," he said. "I am a captain in the Russian army."

"Here is my liberator, my Messiah, a free Jew in uniform," I thought. "God has answered my prayers and given me back my freedom." I was free to walk away and eat, sleep, and talk whenever and wherever I wished.

The officer looked at me—a frail, seventeen year old girl, five feet tall, seventy-five pounds. My hair, which had been shaved off in Auschwitz a year ago, was short and stubby. I wore a pair of mismatched men's shoes. I had stuffed them with rags and paper to keep my feet warm. My dress was torn but I was clean.

"**Meidele*, what is your name?" he asked me.

"Edith."

"Edi..." He could not pronounce it.

"Etu," I tried again, using my Yiddish name.

"Etele?" he asked, using the childish diminutive.

"Yes, Etele," I said and a big smile spread over his face. "What is your name?" I asked him.

"My name is Avrum...Avremele. Tell me, Etele, how is it that you are alive? Are there other Jews who are alive too? Where is your family? Are you alone? How did you survive?" He went on and on with his questions. Finally, he let me talk.

"We were evacuated from our camp by the SS. We marched in the rain twenty to twenty-five miles, day and night, going in circles. Finally, we stopped in a forest. Bombs were falling around us. There was very little food and people died

*little girl

from hunger and cold. Two days ago I left the forest with my friend Irene and we found shelter here in this barn."

"Are there really Jewish people left alive in Europe? You are the first Jew I have met during this long and horrible war," he said.

Irene came out of the barn. She could not talk to Avremele because she only spoke Hungarian. But she was smiling. She sensed that whatever we had been talking about was positive. We were free. We were going home. But we did not know yet that there was no home to go to.

We were quiet for a while. Avremele stroked my cheek gently.

"Etele," he said softly, almost to himself, "I had a little sister your age who was killed by the Germans. You remind me of her." He put his hand in his pocket and pulled out a bar of soap. "Please, take it. I don't have anything else to give you. I have to leave now."

I held the precious soap. I wondered if he knew how much I had missed this soap last night and all the times before. I watched him walk away to join his troops. Suddenly he turned around. "Etele, take care of yourself."

I waved goodbye until he disappeared into his unit and prayed to God to watch over Avremele.

It was the morning of May 8, 1945.

After The War

LILLY, MOTHER AND EDITH, 1946

MONUMENT IN MEMORY OF THE VICTIMS
OF THE HOLOCAUST FROM CHUST (HUST), ISRAEL

Epilogue

I said goodbye to Avremele and never saw him again. Irene and I moved into the farmhouse. We stayed in this village for two weeks. The Russians ordered the German villagers to give the survivors food, clothing and shelter. We ate as much as we could and drank a bucket of milk a day. When we felt strong enough, we began the journey back home.

Because of the chaos right after the war there were no train schedules and anyone could get on a train without paying. But travel was very slow.

We stopped in Prague looking for relatives. I was told by a friend of the family, also a survivor, that my mother was alive and waiting in Chust. I could not believe it! We continued on to

Budapest where Irene and I went our separate ways.

It took me more than two weeks to reach Chust, a trip that should have taken two days. Finally, I came home to my mother. The next day Lilly arrived unexpectedly. Our joy was indescribable. We felt our lives were beginning again.

We waited for my father and brother but they never came back. They did not survive the Holocaust. My father was forty-three years old. My brother was eighteen.

We left Chust because we wanted to get out of Europe. The only way out was through Germany, as the rest of Eastern Europe was under Communist control.

We found ourselves in Heidenheim, Germany, in a Displaced Persons' Camp where we waited for emigration papers. The United States had a quota system which involved years of waiting. Israel was still under the British Mandate and we could not enter legally.

In Heidenheim, I met another Jewish, Russian officer named Michael—and this one I married. He too lost his family in the Holocaust. We left for Israel as part of the last illegal *Aliyah* in 1948.

Israel's War of Independence was going on. Michael was immediately drafted and was fighting in a war once again. In 1956 he fought in the Sinai Campaign.

My daughters Ester and Shula were born in Israel. A few years later, we moved to Los Angeles.

Michael and I went back to school to complete our education which had been interrupted by the war. Michael received his Ph.D. in history. I got my teaching credentials and have been teaching since 1965.

We are blessed to have our daughters and four grandchildren all living near us.

Lilly lives in Israel with her family. My mother also lived in Israel until she died peacefully in her sleep at the age of eighty-two.

*Immigration to Israel

Acknowledgements

With special thanks to my husband and best friend, Michael, who encouraged me to write.

To my daughter, Shula who spent countless hours editing and typing my stories.

To my daughter, Ester who coordinated the publishing of this book.

And to Jim Zuckerman who gave of his time and photographic talents.